PEANUTS
Happiness Is Having a Friend

A FILL-IN BOOK

RP **STUDIO**

PHILADELPHIA

You're a good friend,

~~~~~~~~~~~~~~~~~~~~~~~~~~~~~~~~~~~~~

IF WE WERE PEANUTS CHARACTERS, I'D BE

~~~~~~ ,

AND YOU'D DEFINITELY BE

~~~~~~ .

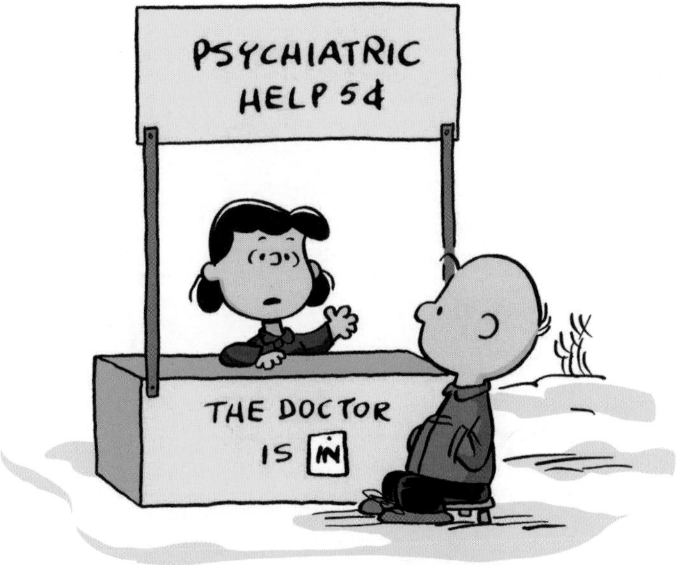
PSYCHIATRIC HELP 5¢
THE DOCTOR IS IN

THE BEST ADVICE YOU EVER GAVE ME AS A FRIEND WAS

_____ .

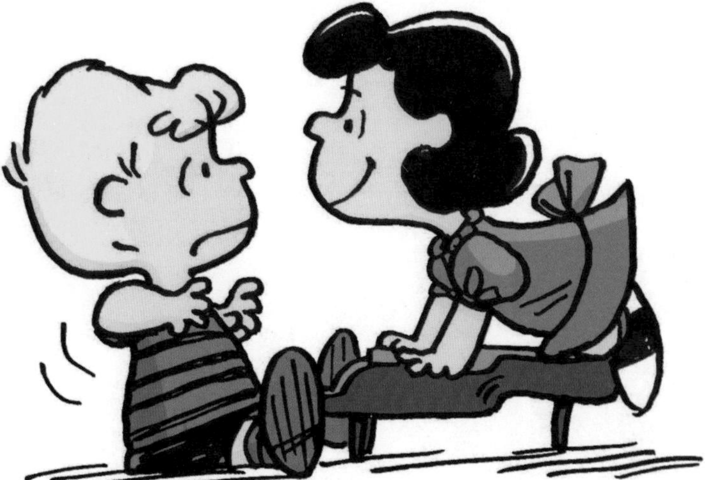

IF SCHROEDER WROTE A SONG ABOUT OUR FRIENDSHIP, IT WOULD BE TITLED

〜〜〜〜〜〜〜〜〜〜〜〜〜〜〜〜〜〜〜〜〜〜〜〜〜 .

GOOD GRIEF! I CAN'T BELIEVE WE'VE BEEN FRIENDS FOR

~~~~~~ .

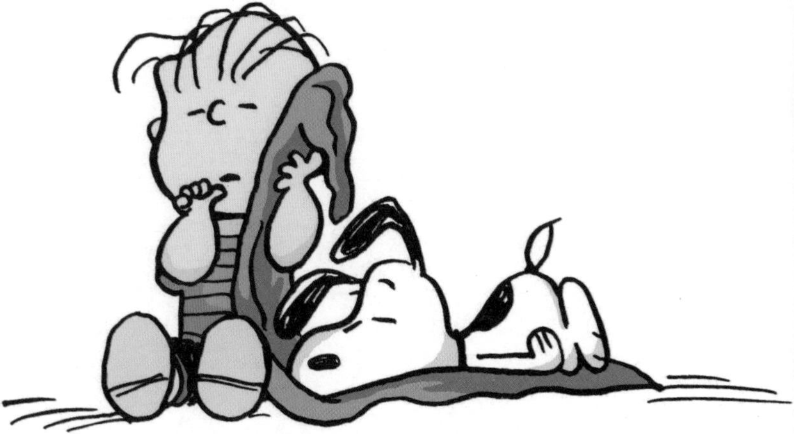

Like Linus' security blanket, you're always

~~~~~~ .

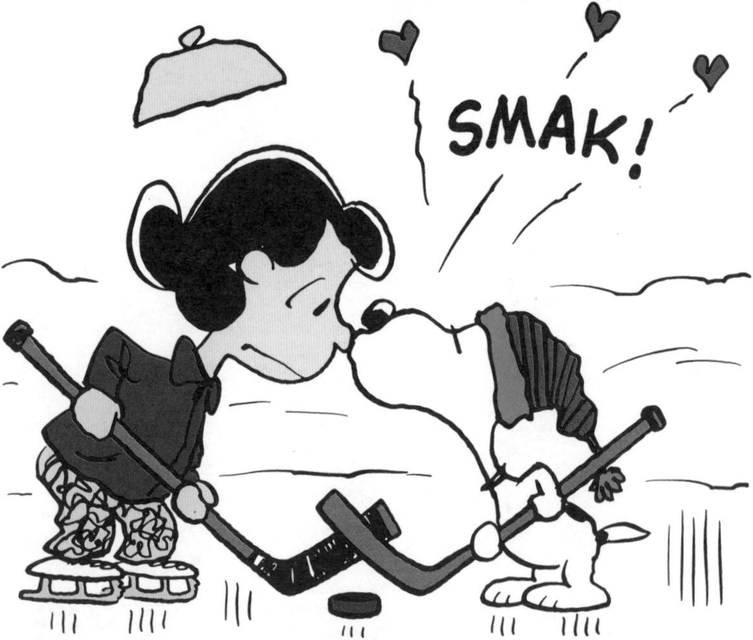
SMAK!

LUCY SAYS, "HAPPINESS IS A WARM PUPPY," BUT FRIENDSHIP IS

〰〰〰〰〰〰〰〰〰〰〰〰〰〰〰〰〰〰〰〰〰〰〰〰〰 .

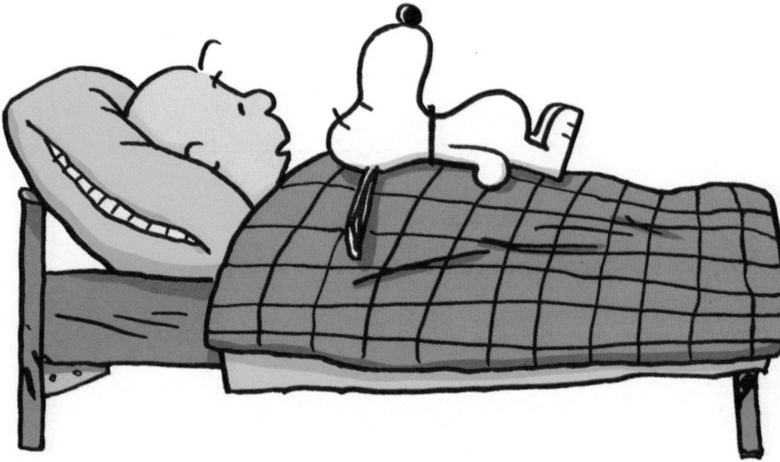

LAST NIGHT I DREAMT THAT WE

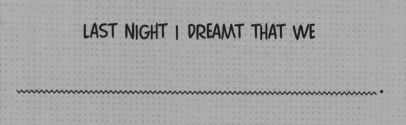

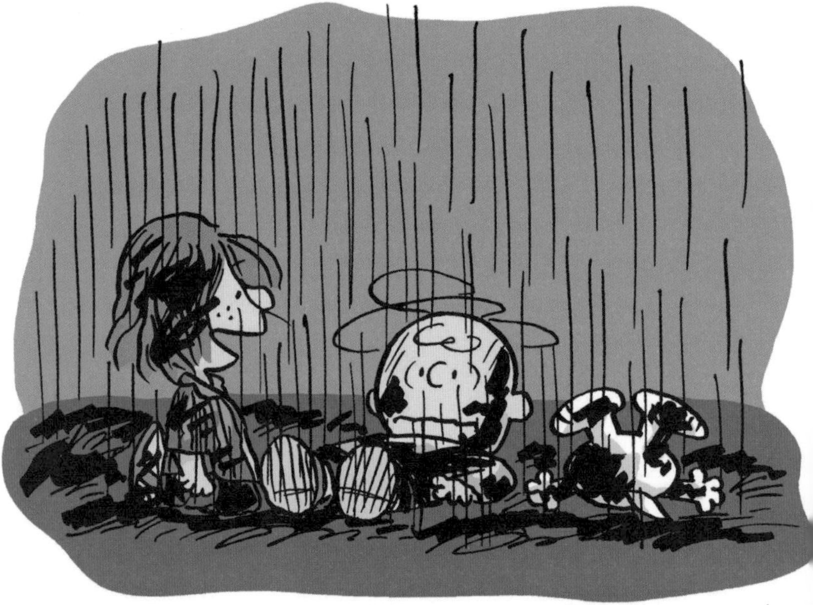

I'LL ALWAYS BE THERE FOR YOU, COME
RAIN OR SHINE OR

〰〰〰〰〰〰〰〰〰〰〰〰〰〰〰〰〰〰〰〰〰〰〰〰〰〰〰〰〰〰.

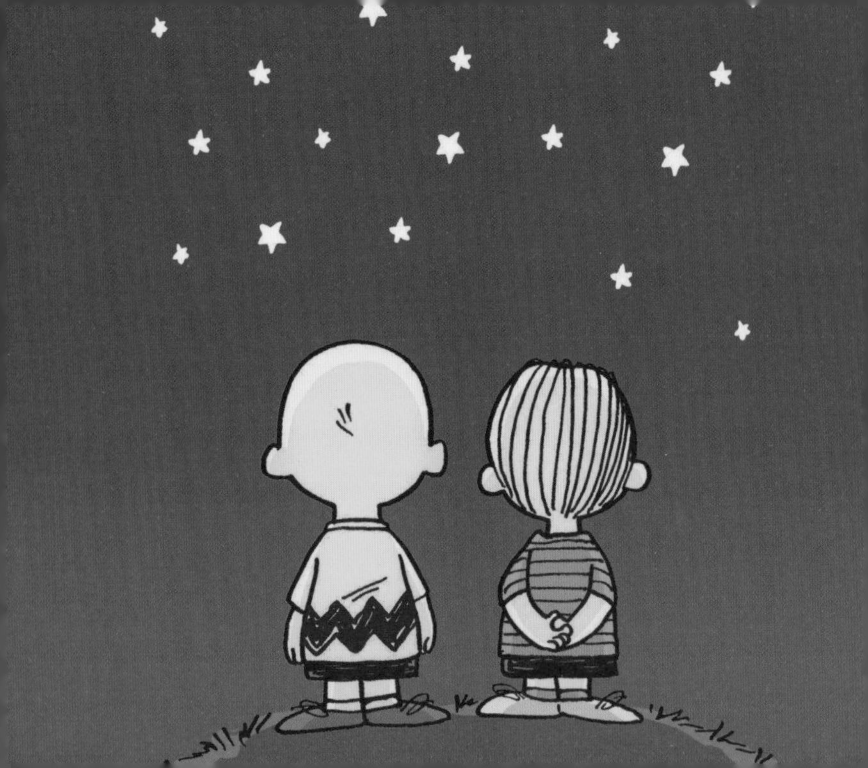

IN THE ENORMITY OF THE UNIVERSE OUR FRIENDSHIP IS

〜〜〜〜〜〜〜〜〜〜〜〜〜〜〜〜〜〜〜〜〜〜〜〜 .

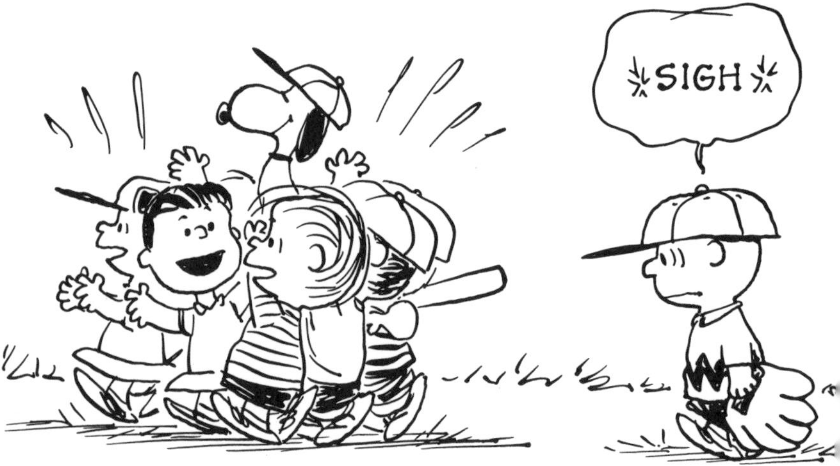
SIGH

I'LL ALWAYS BE YOUR NUMBER ONE FAN, EVEN IF

____.

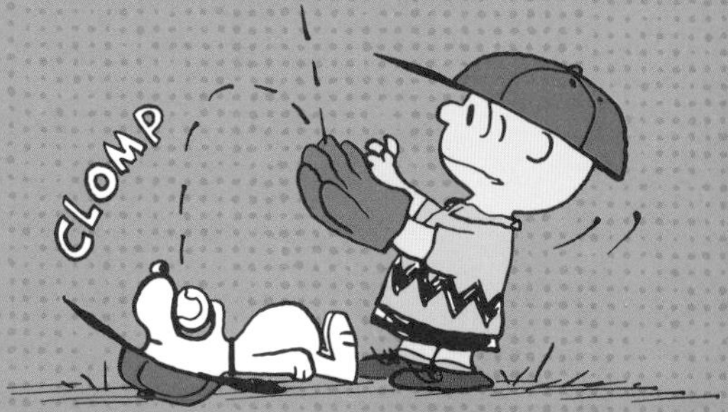
CLOMP

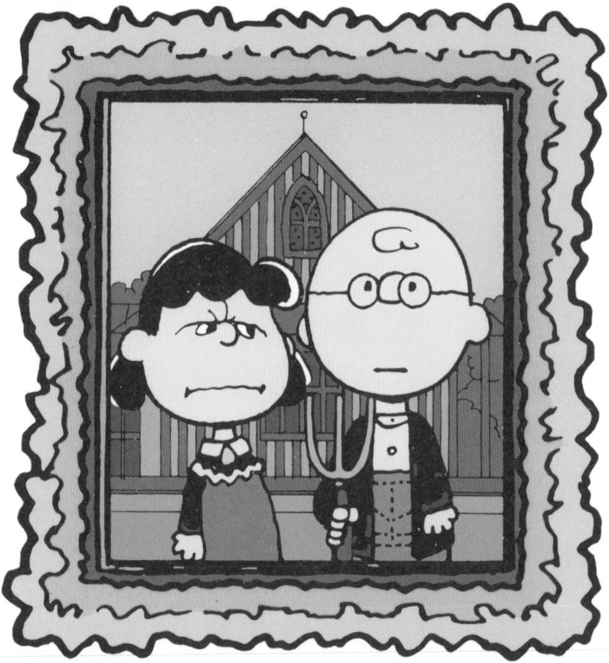

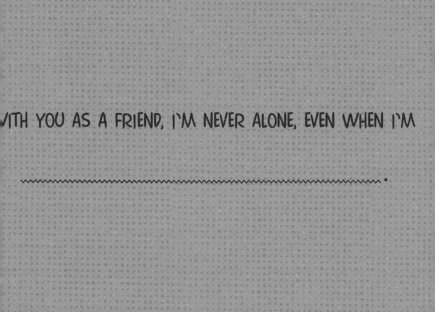
WITH YOU AS A FRIEND, I'M NEVER ALONE, EVEN WHEN I'M

~~~~~~~~~~~~~~~~~~~~~~~~~~~~~~~~~~~~ .

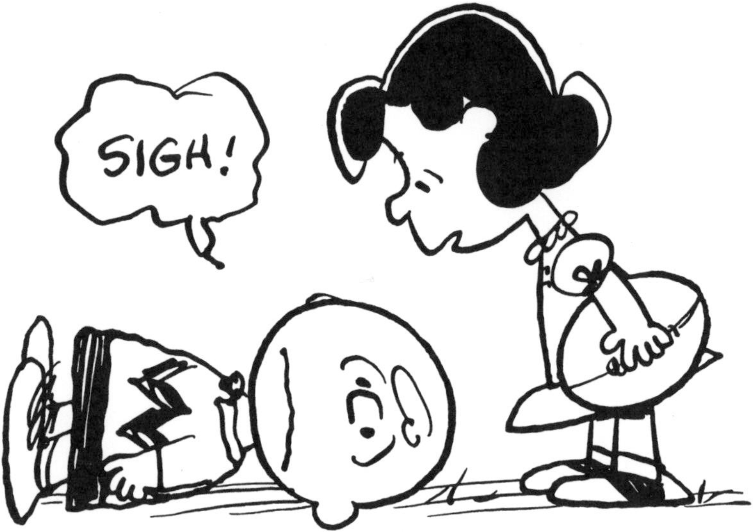
SIGH!

Every time I think of our

~~~~~~,

I *SIGH*.

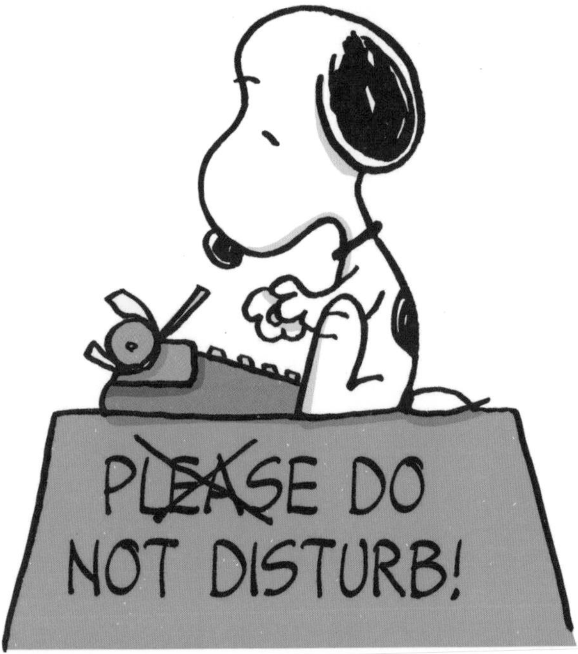
PLEASE DO
NOT DISTURB!

"IT WAS A DARK AND STORMY NIGHT" WHEN WE

‿‿‿‿‿‿‿‿‿‿‿‿‿‿‿‿‿‿‿‿‿‿‿‿‿‿‿‿‿‿‿‿‿‿‿‿‿‿‿ .

YOU ACCEPT ME FOR WHO I AM,

~~~~~~

AND ALL.

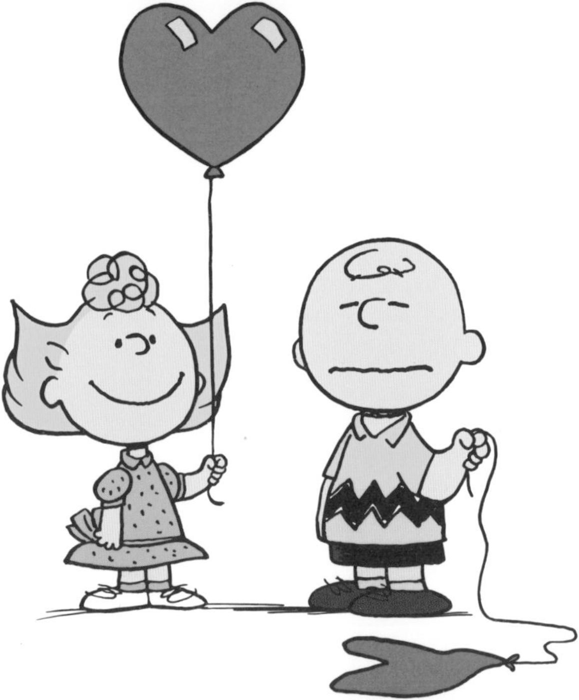

BESIDES FRIENDSHIP, THE BEST THING
YOU EVER GAVE ME WAS

〰〰〰〰〰〰〰〰〰〰〰〰〰〰〰〰〰〰〰〰〰〰〰〰〰〰〰 .

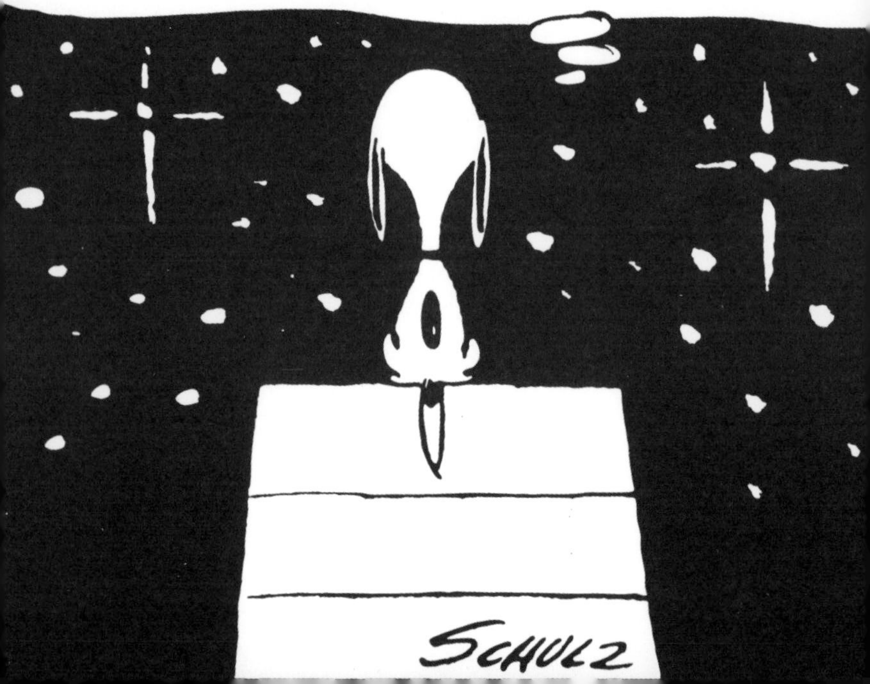
SCHULZ

Sometimes I lie awake at night, and I ask if our friendship will

〜〜〜〜〜〜〜〜〜〜〜〜〜〜〜〜〜〜〜〜〜 ·

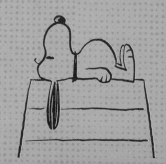

IF SALLY WROTE AN ENGLISH THEME
ABOUT OUR FRIENDSHIP, SHE WOULD TITLE IT

" _____ ".

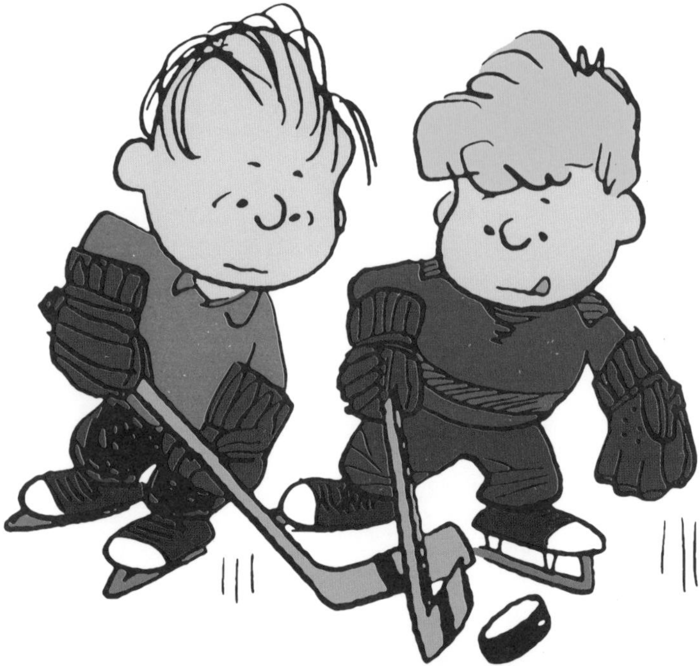

THAT'S THE SECRET OF FRIENDSHIP...

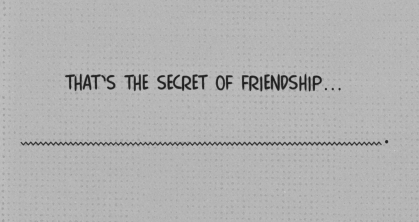

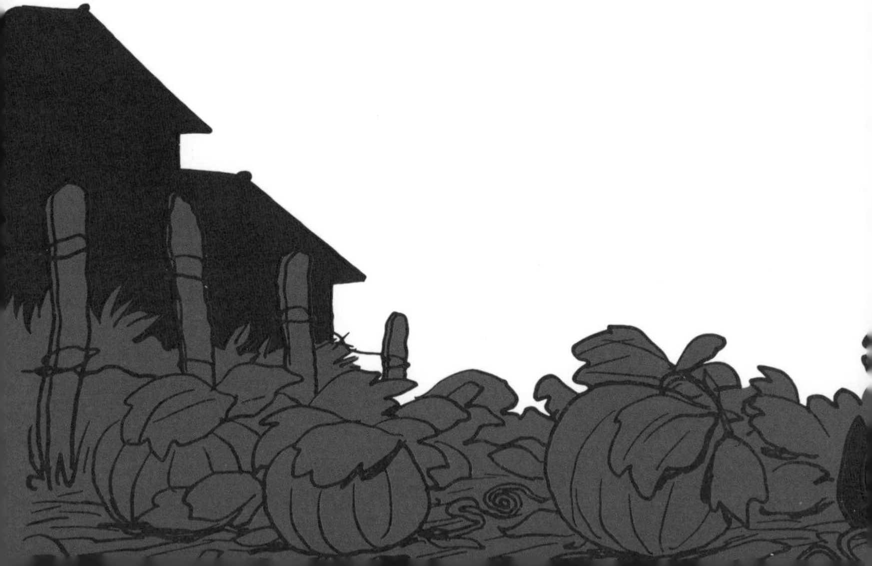

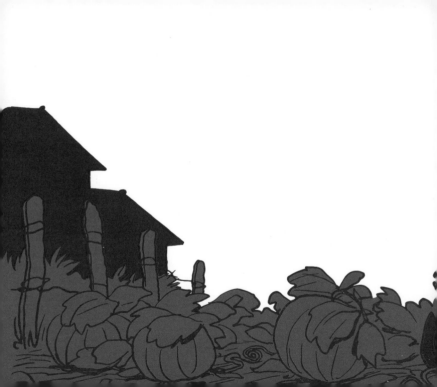

JUST WAIT UNTIL NEXT YEAR! TOGETHER, WE WILL

________________________________.

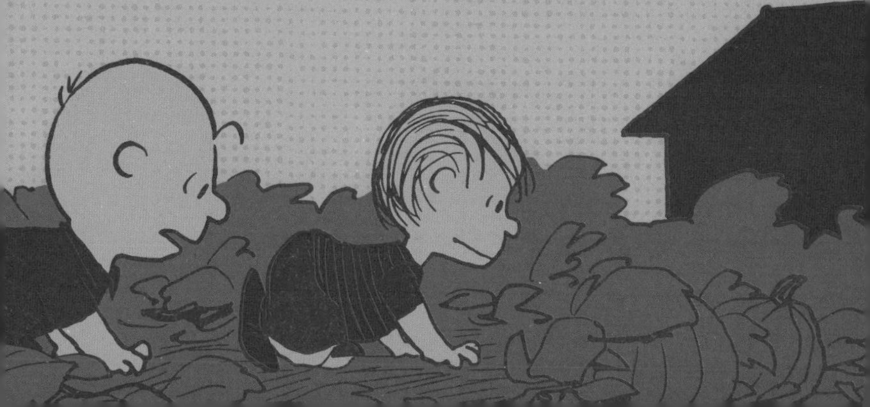

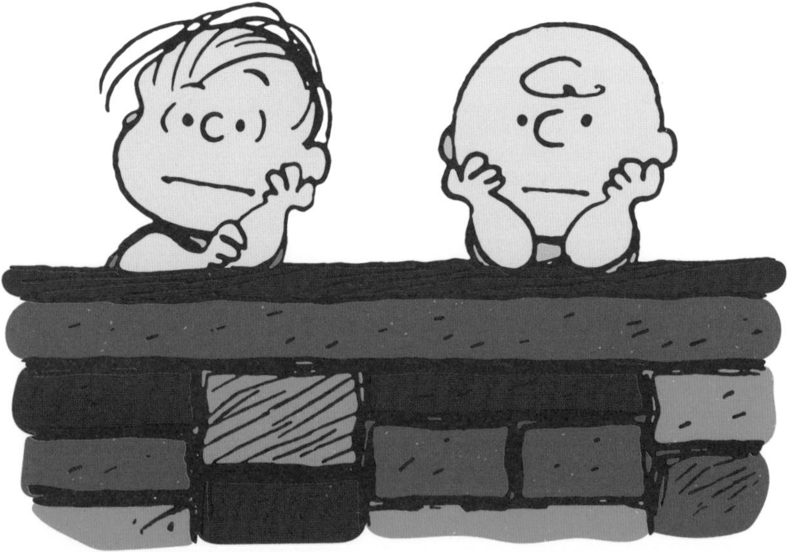

WHEN I'M IN MY "DEPRESSED STANCE," YOU KNOW

~~~~~~

ALWAYS CHEERS ME UP.

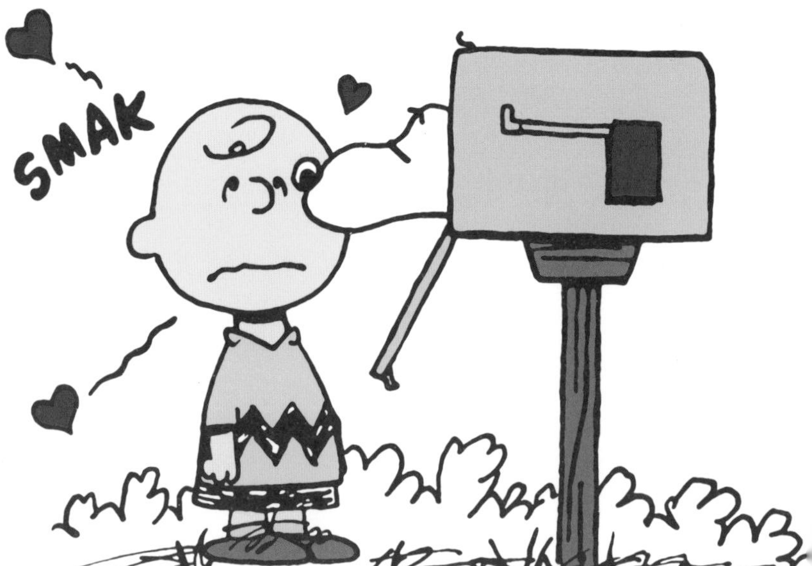
SMAK

Yesterday I was your friend. Today I'm your friend. Tomorrow I'll probably still be ~~~~~~ .

I HATE MYSELF FOR NOT HAVING ENOUGH
NERVE TO TELL YOU

〜〜〜〜〜〜〜〜〜〜〜〜〜〜〜〜〜〜〜〜〜〜〜〜〜 .

WE MAY NOT KNOW "BIRD SPEAK" LIKE WOODSTOCK,
WE HAVE OUR OWN SPECIAL LANGUAGE CALLED

〰〰〰〰〰〰〰〰〰〰〰〰〰〰〰〰 .

AS MY BEST FRIEND, YOU KNOW MY WORST FEAR IS

~~~~~~ ,

AND I KNOW YOURS IS

~~~~~~ .

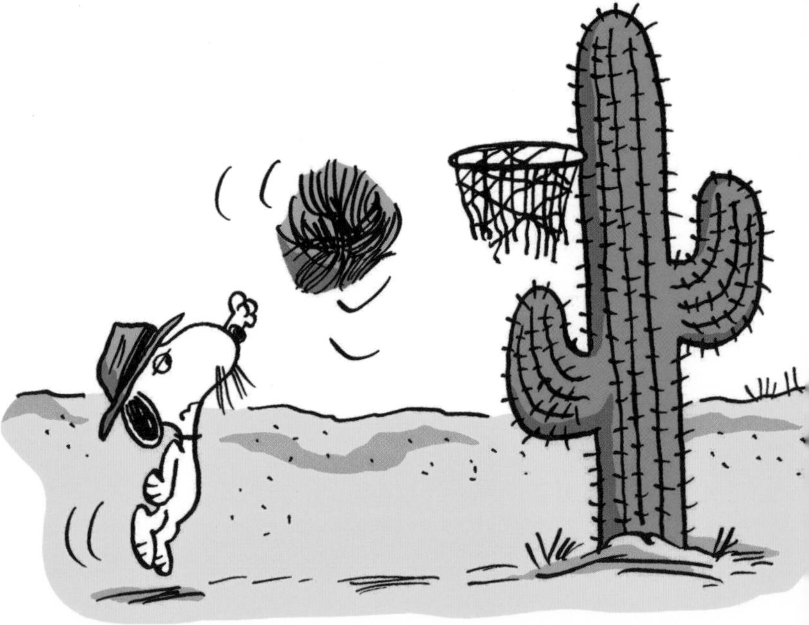

IF YOU AND I WERE LOST IN THE DESERT, THE
ONLY THING WE'D NEED IS

~~~~~~ .

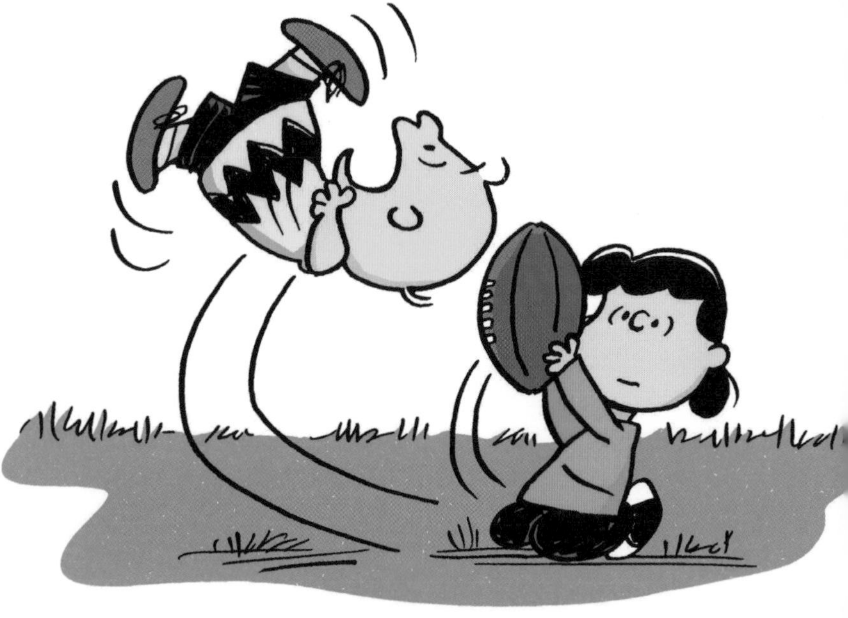

No matter how many times you

~~~~~~ ,

I'll always trust you wholeheartedly.

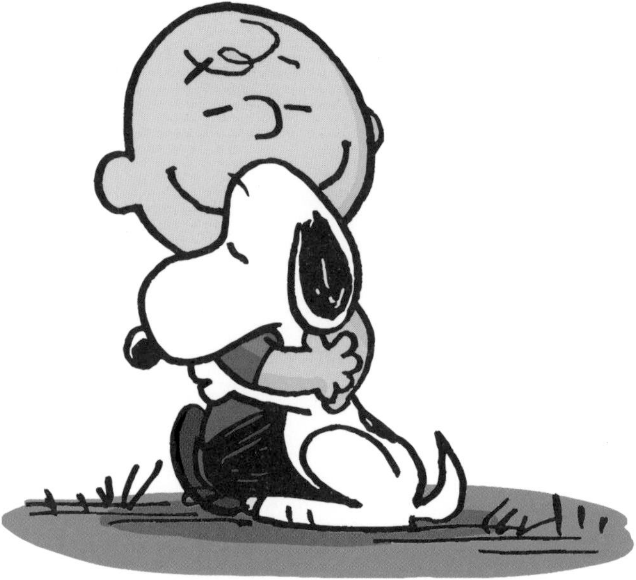

...Y MIND REELS WITH SARCASTIC REPLIES, WHENEVER YOU

~~~~~~ .

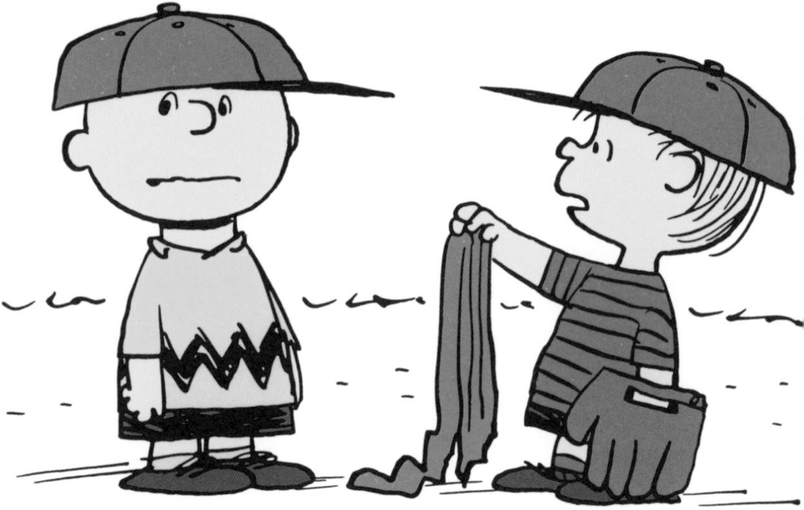

I LOVE ALL MANKIND—BUT YOU ARE MY

〰〰〰〰〰〰〰〰〰〰〰〰〰〰〰〰〰〰〰〰〰〰〰〰 !

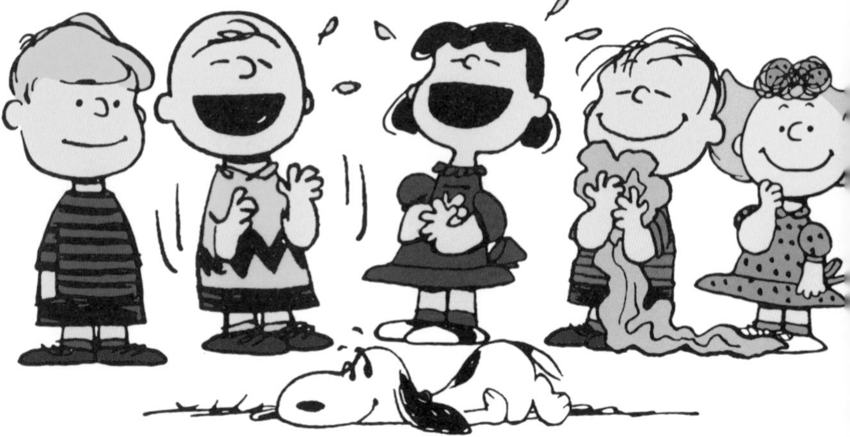

YOU MAKE ME LAUGH, ESPECIALLY WHEN

〜〜〜〜〜〜〜〜〜〜〜〜〜〜〜〜〜〜〜〜〜 .

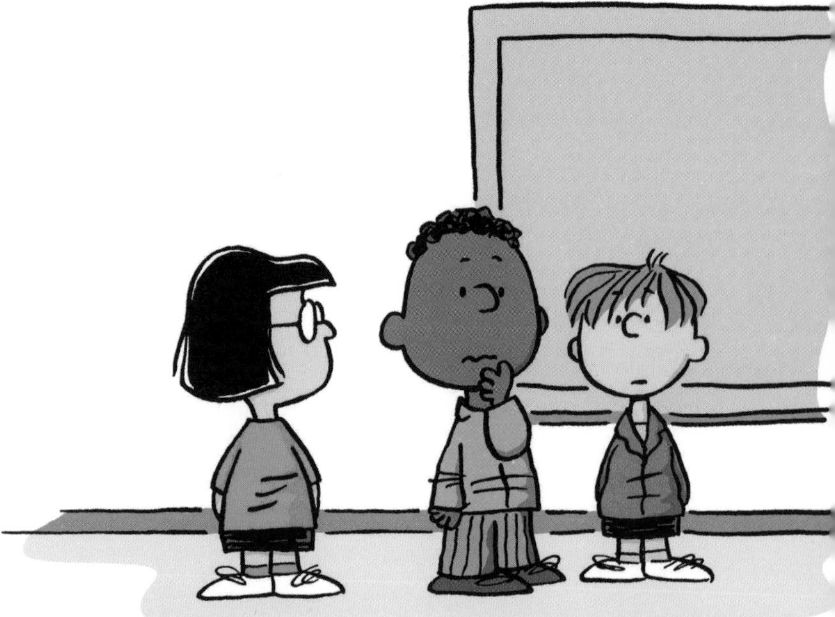

IF WE HAD A SHOW-AND-TELL, I WOULD BRING

~~~~~~

TO REPRESENT OUR FRIENDSHIP.

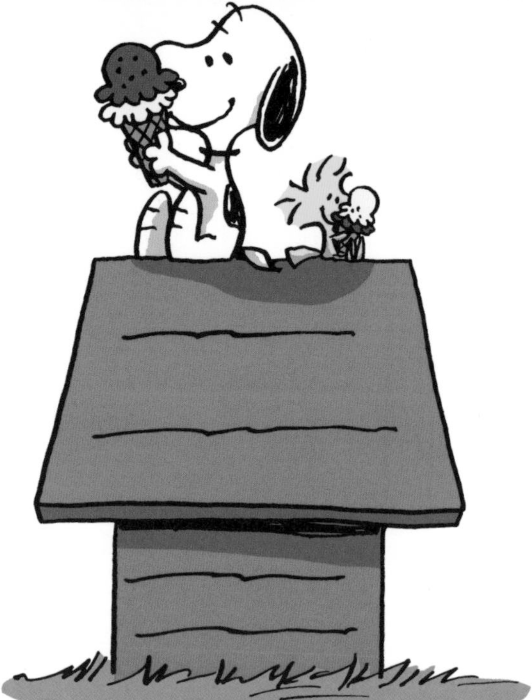

A FRIEND IS SOMEONE WHO LOVES YOU IN SPITE OF

〜〜〜〜〜〜〜〜〜〜〜〜〜〜〜〜〜〜〜〜〜〜 .

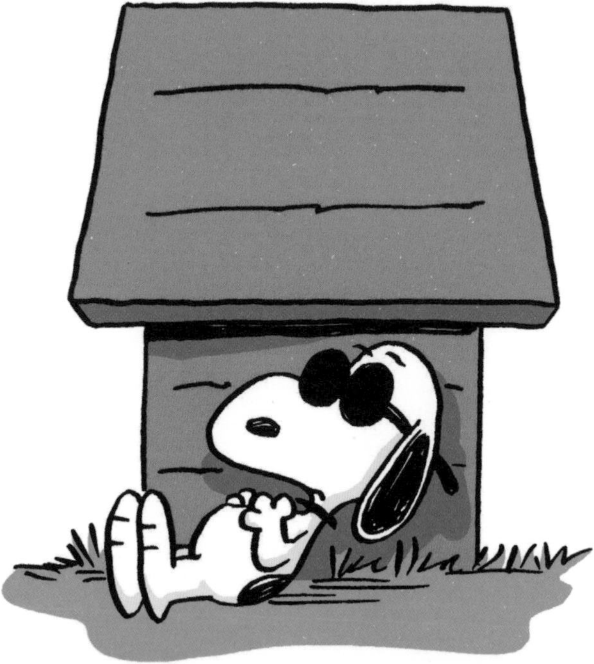

NOT EVEN JOE COOL IS AS

~~~~~~

AS YOU.

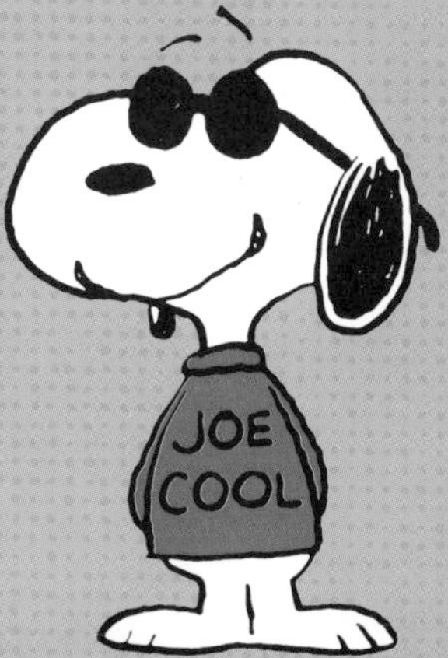
JOE
COOL
~~~~~~

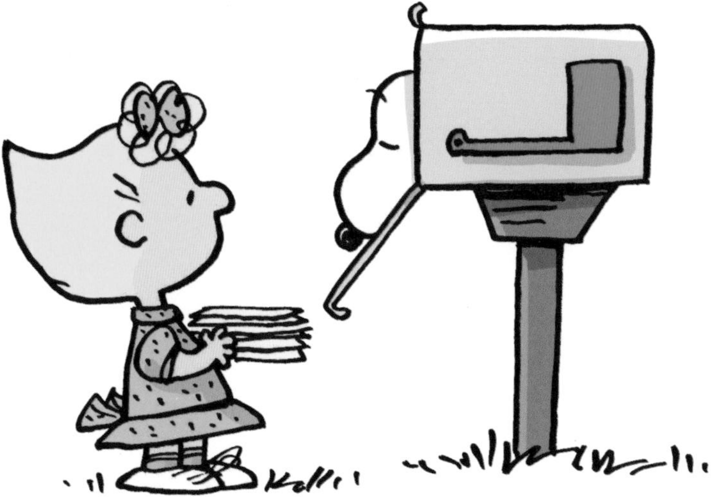

WHEN IT COMES TO OUR FRIENDSHIP, ABSENCE MAKES THE HEART GROW FONDER, BUT IT SURE MAKES THE REST OF ME

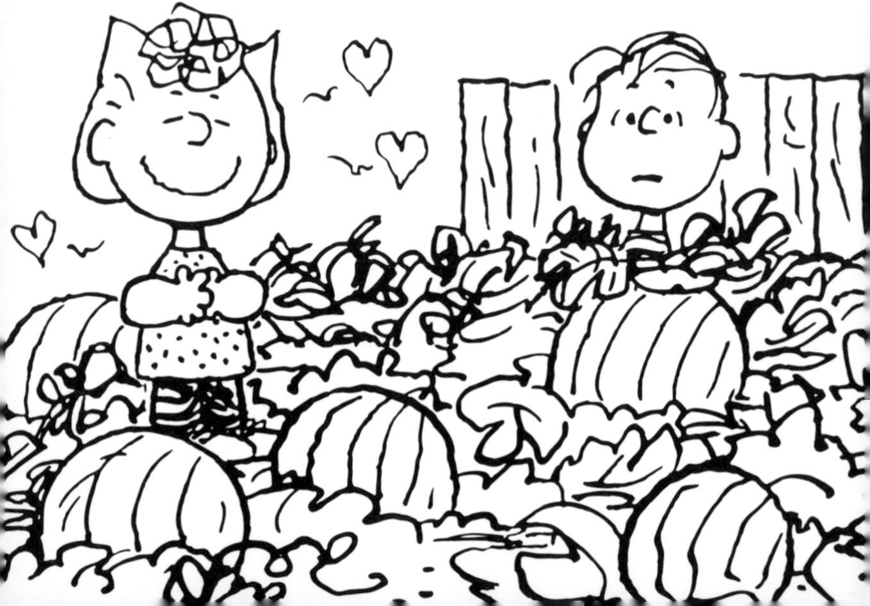

IF LINUS IS SALLY'S "SWEET BABBOO,"
YOU'RE DEFINITELY MY

〰〰〰〰〰〰〰〰〰〰〰〰〰〰〰〰〰〰〰〰 .

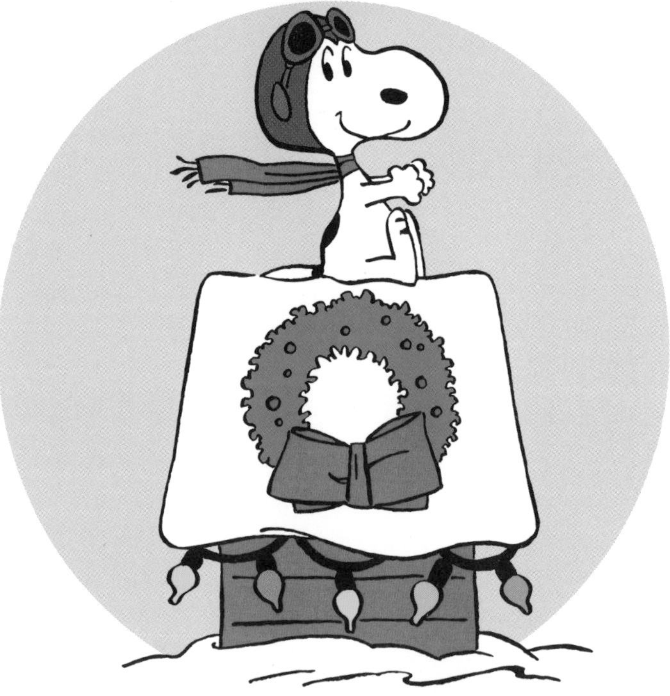

IF WE COULD FLY WITH THE RED BARON,
I WOULD TRAVEL TO

_____,

WHILE YOU'D DEFINITELY GO TO

_____.

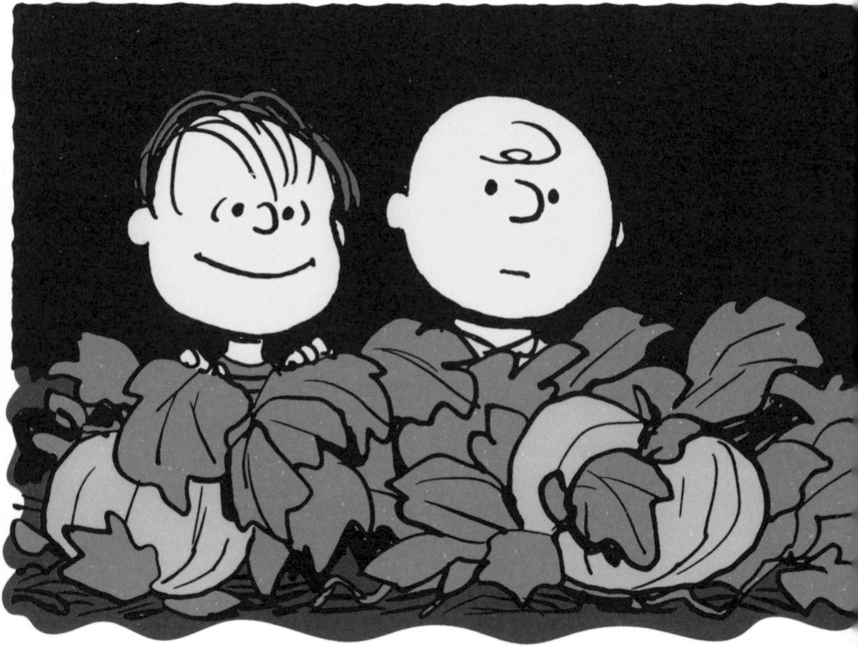

Even when we're doing nothing special
together, it's always

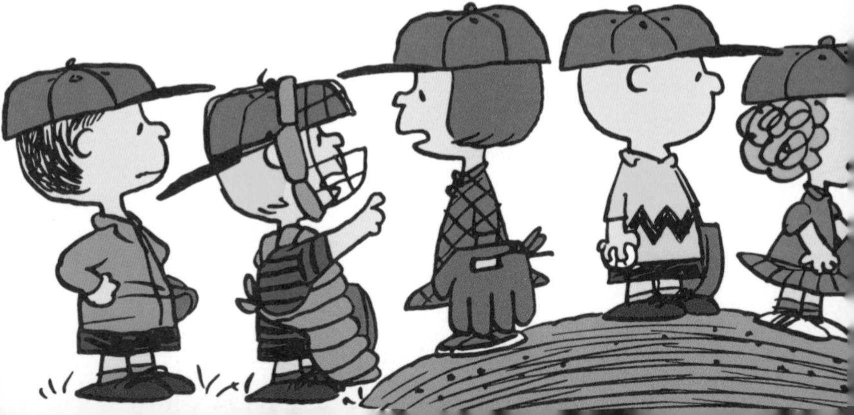

IF WE PLAYED ON CHARLIE BROWN'S BASEBALL TEAM, I'D DEFINITELY PLAY THE

~~~~~~,

POSITION, AND YOU'D BE THE

~~~~~~.

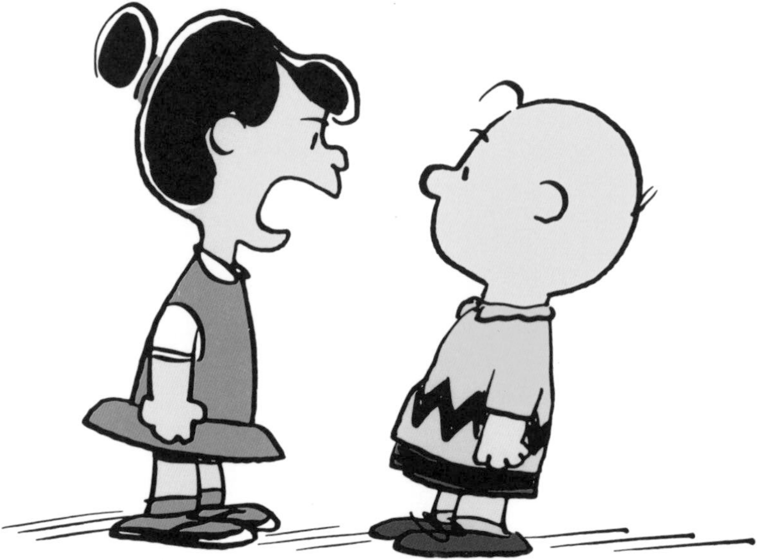

WE WERE TOTAL BLOCKHEADS THAT ONE TIME WE

~~~~~~ .

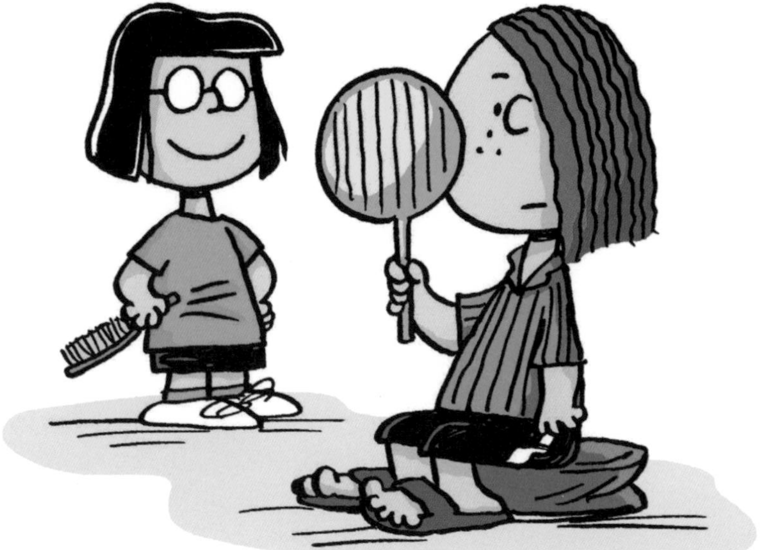

I BET IF WE NEVER MET, I'D BE

\~ .

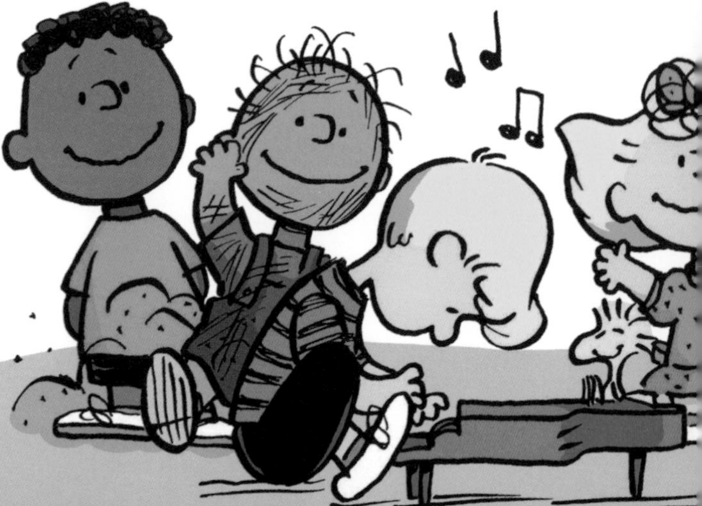

SCHROEDER SAYS, "THE JOY IS IN THE PLAYING," WHICH PERFECTLY DESCRIBES WHEN WE

____.

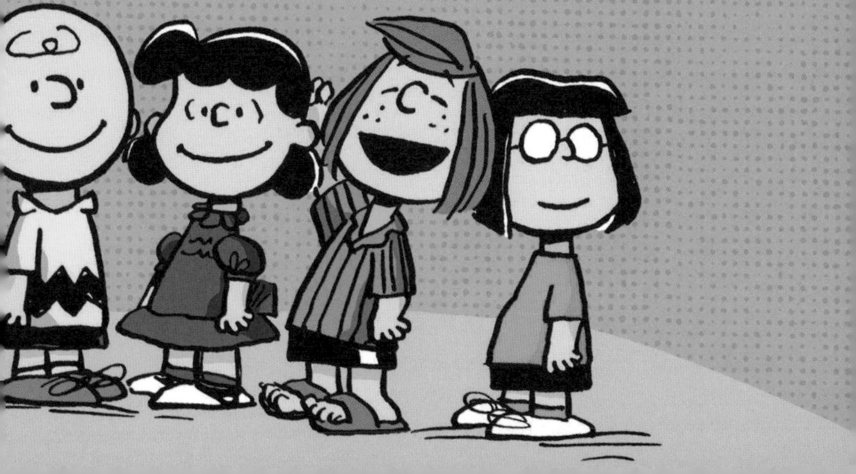

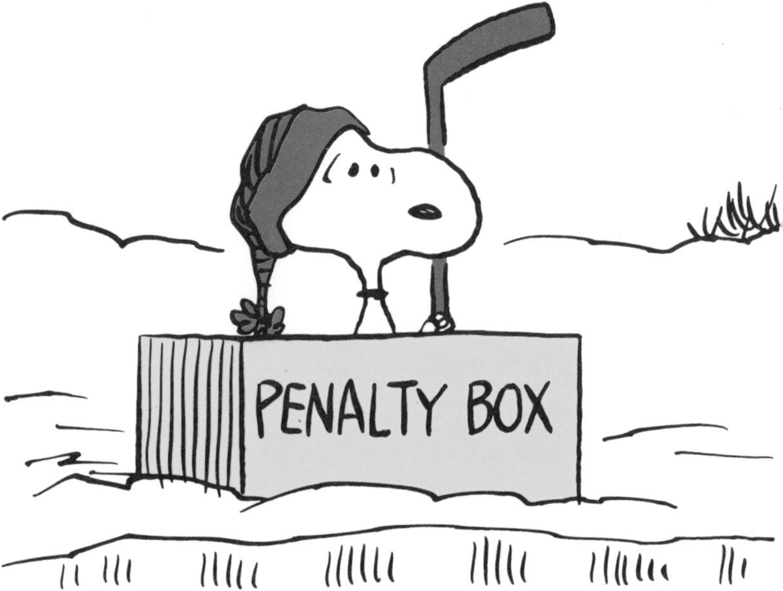
PENALTY BOX

AS MY FRIEND, YOU KNOW I JUST CAN'T STAND

~~~~~~.

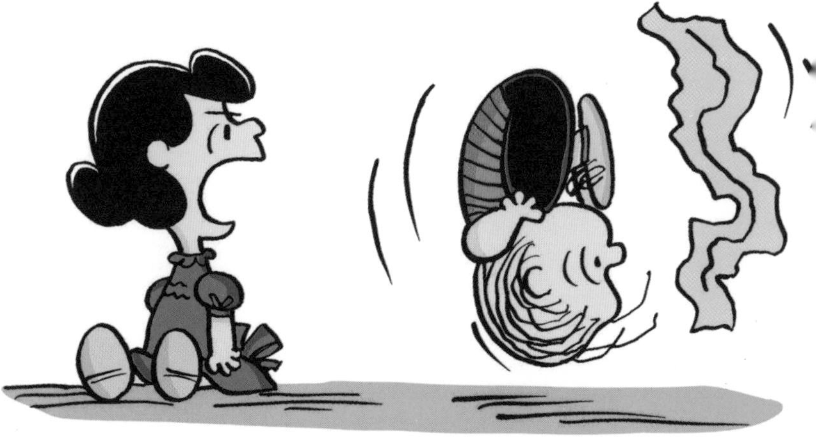

WE DON'T FIGHT OFTEN, BUT I OUGHTA
CLOBBER YOU WHEN

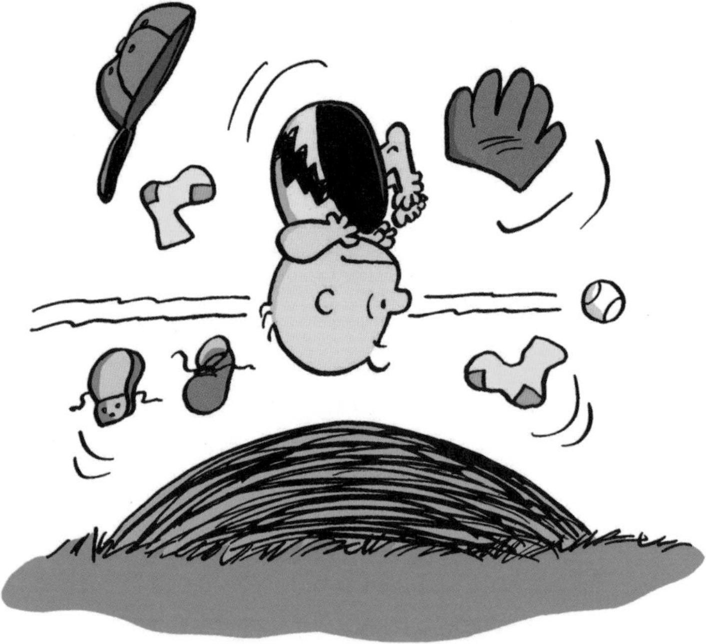

No matter what, you're always a
good sport, even when

〜〜〜〜〜〜〜〜〜〜〜〜〜〜〜〜〜〜〜〜〜〜〜〜〜〜 .

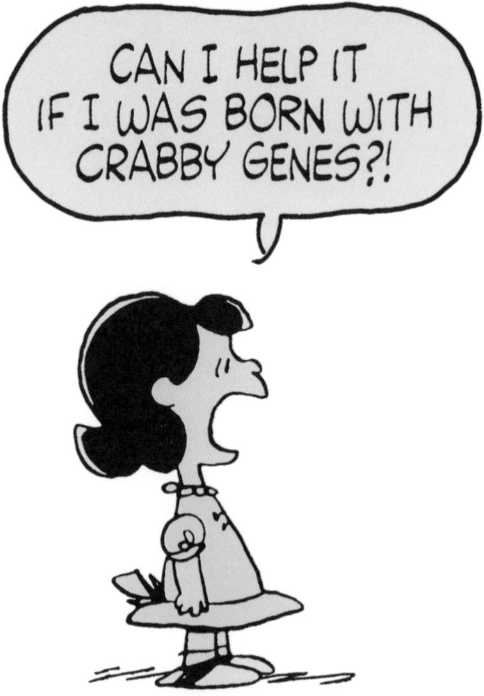
CAN I HELP IT IF I WAS BORN WITH CRABBY GENES?!

NO ONE UNDERSTANDS US

~~~~~~~~~~~~~~~~~~~~~~~~~~~~~~~~

PEOPLE!

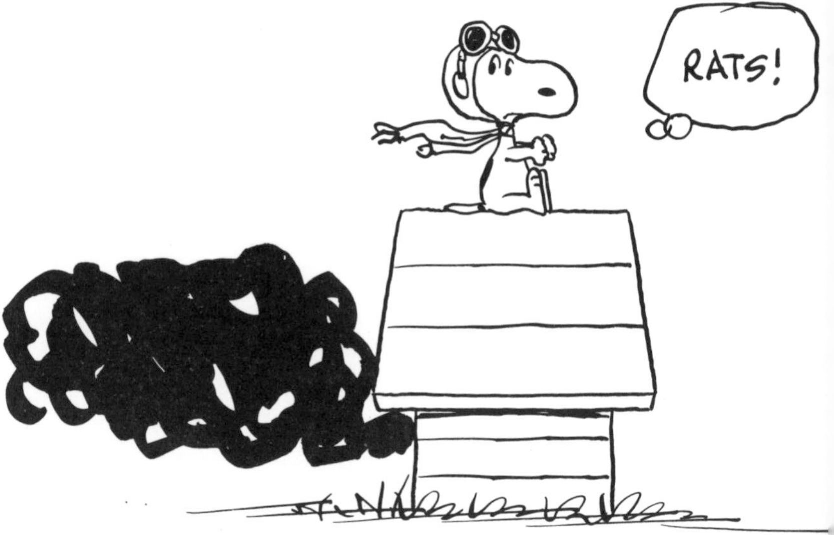
RATS!

"RATS!" THIS BOOK MAY BE FINISHED, BUT OUR FRIENDSHIP IS

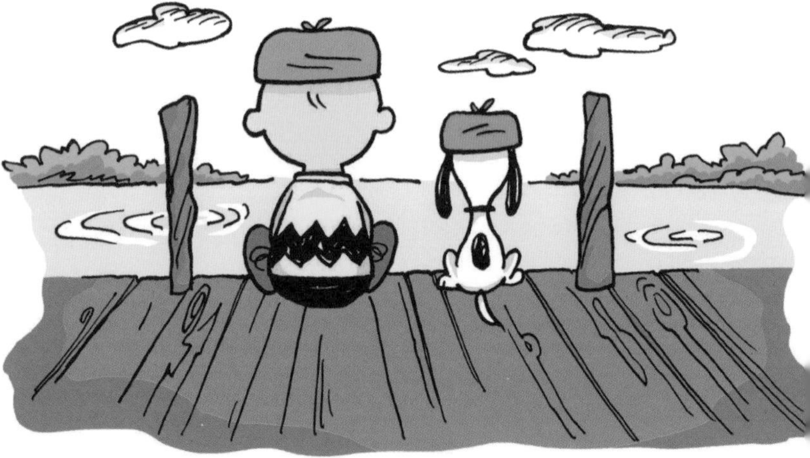

RP Studio™
Hachette Book Group
1290 Avenue of the Americas, New York, NY 10104
www.runningpress.com
@Running_Press

Printed in China

First Edition: May 2021

Published by RP Studio, an imprint of Perseus Books, LLC, a subsidiary of Hachette Book
Group, Inc. The RP Studio name and logo is a trademark of the Hachette Book Group.

The publisher is not responsible for websites (or their content) that are not owned by the publisher.

Design by Celeste Joyce

This book is inspired by the comic strip Peanuts by Charles M. Schulz.

Art by Charles M. Schulz & Vicki Scott

ISBN: 978-0-7624-9913-7

1010

10 9 8 7 6 5 4 3 2 1